CW01083569

49 Excuses for Being Really Late

Copyright © 2016, 2022 by James Warwood

Published by Curious Squirrel Press

Book cover design by: James Warwood
Book interior design by: Mala Letra / Lic. Sara F. Salomon

ISBN: 9798436064857
ebook ISBN: B0IM8FJ5PU

THE EXCUSE ENCYCLOPEDIA

Book Seven:
49 Excuses for Being
Really Late

James Warwood

BOOK SEVEN

Excuses for Being Really Late

LATE EXCUSES

1. THE GOOD MORNING EXCUSE

Isn't it such a wonderful morning .

. .

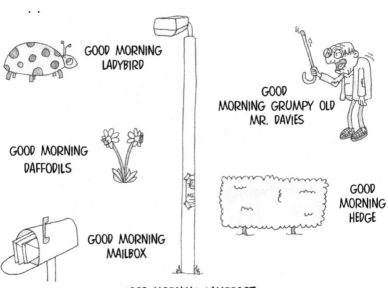

GOOD MORNING LADYBIRD

GOOD MORNING GRUMPY OLD MR. DAVIES

GOOD MORNING DAFFODILS

GOOD MORNING HEDGE

GOOD MORNING MAILBOX

GOOD MORNING LAMPPOST

. . . I had to stop and say good morning to everything and everyone I met on my wonderful walk to school this morning.

(Once you've listed everything you can think of, finish by saying "good morning" to your teacher.)

2. THE THINKING EXCUSE

I admit to being late this morning . . .

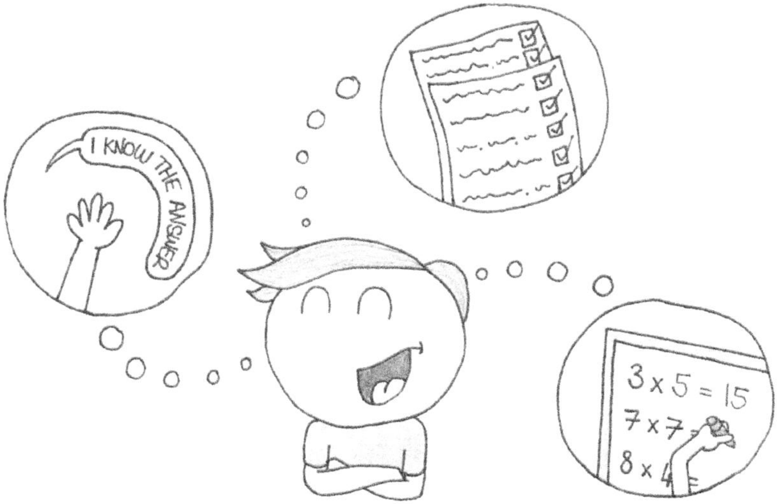
I KNOW THE ANSWER
3 x 5 = 15
7 x 7
8 x 4

. . . But I promise I was thinking about school the whole time.

3. THE LITTLE MISS LATE EXCUSE

Do you like my fancy dress costume

. . .

. . . I'm going to a friend's birthday party as *Little Miss Late*. So I decided to put on my costume this morning and get into character.

4. THE SNOOZE BUTTON EXCUSE

Sorry I'm late. I slept in, again . . .

. . . I blame the snooze button. It always taunts me in the morning. Well, this morning I managed to defeat it once and for all! Does anyone know where I can buy an alarm clock without a snooze button?

5. THE SHORT-CUT EXCUSE

Sorry I'm late . . .

. . . That's the last time I decide to take a short-cut through the local building site!

6. THE TEN MINUTE SILENCE EXCUSE

I accidentally dropped my breakfast on the floor this morning . . .

. . . So I held a 10 minute silence in honour of this terrible tragedy and loss of nutritional life. R.I.P. jam on toast. I'll never forget you.

7. THE CAT FIGHT EXCUSE

My cat got in a fight at 2am . . .

. . . So I had to teach him a valuable lesson about waking up his owner in the early hours of the morning. I hope you'll agree that Gizmo has learnt his lesson.

8. THE JEALOUS PILLOWS EXCUSE

Really sorry I'm late, but my pillows suffer from Separation Anxiety . . .

. . . They have grown so attached to me that they can't function as law-abiding pillows without being close to me. Now I have to take them with me everywhere I go.

9. THE WRONG BIKE EXCUSE

My bike had a flat tyre this morning, so I borrowed my mum's bike . . .

. . . After cycling 20 miles I realised it was an aerobic bike. But on the bright side I lost three pounds!

10. THE BEAUTY SLEEP EXCUSE

Look, I know I'm late - *again* - but have you seen my face? . . .

. . . I desperately need extra beauty sleep. If you don't believe me I can get a doctor's note. My mum is a doctor and she screams and then hides behind a chair every time I walk into the room.

11. THE WONDERLAND EXCUSE

I was walking to school when I accidentally fell down a rabbit hole . . .

. . . Then I had a lovely tea party with some odd but nice people. Yes, I did just read Alice in Wonderland. How did you know that?

12. THE WATCH RESET EXCUSE

What? It's 9:35am! That's odd, my watch says 8:45am . . .

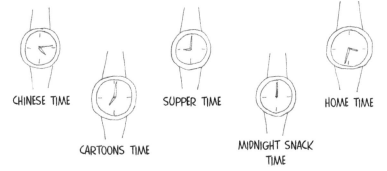

CHINESE TIME

CARTOONS TIME

SUPPER TIME

MIDNIGHT SNACK TIME

HOME TIME

. . . Although come to think of it I did adjust my watch forward by 8 hours to see what time it was in China, then adjust the time back to 7am so I could watch cartoons, then adjust the time forward to 9pm so I could have supper, then adjust the time forward by 3 hours so I could have a midnight snack, then adjust the time back to 3:30pm so I could pretend it was home time. What's the time again?

13. THE NEW INVENTION EXCUSE

I've invented a brand new mode of transport. Behold! *The Solar-Powered Monster Truck* . . .

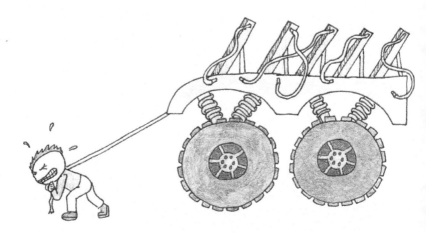

. . . Unfortunately, being solar-powered, it stopped halfway to school when it started to rain. I had to pull it the rest of the way. Maybe I could build a *Rain-Powered Monster Truck* during the Geography lesson later?

14. THE CLEAN EXCUSE

I had to have 3 showers this morning . . .

. . . Let me explain. I had my morning shower and then walked into a spider's web. Then I had another shower and then slipped on a banana skin and fell into the bin. Then I had another shower and then fell in a muddy puddle at the school entrance. But at least I'm clean.

15. THE WRONG MAP EXCUSE

The new school layout is far too confusing . . .

. . . I keep on getting lost! I think I'm in Adventureland because I've walked past Space Mountain and dodged Buzz Lightyear's Astro Blasters. I can now see Tarzan's Treehouse and the Pirate's Lair on Tom Sawyer Island in the distance. Is my new classroom in the big, fancy castle?

16. THE NEW SHOES EXCUSE

I bought these new protective shoes . . .

. . . I didn't realise that they are made from concrete, lead and osmium (the heaviest metal in the world).

17. THE LONELY GOLDFISH EXCUSE

I just couldn't leave my house this morning . . .

. . . It's Seaweed's fault. Look at him. I'd like to see you try and leave my goldfish while he is giving you the *don't leave me again* look.

18. THE HEADTEACHER EXCUSE

Sorry I am late, but I just had a wonderful conversation with the Headteacher . . .

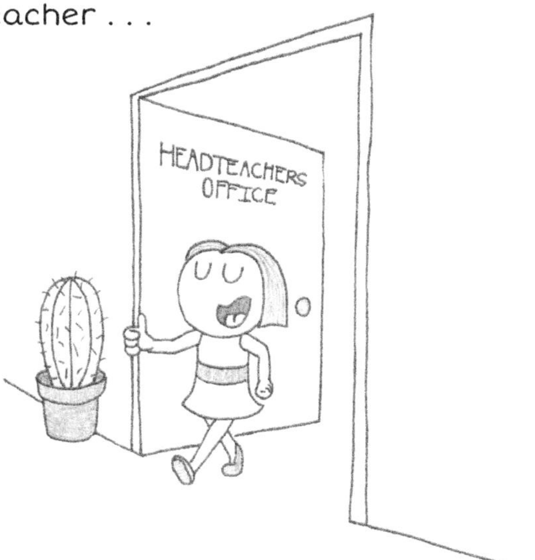
HEADTEACHERS
OFFICE

. . . We discussed your career progression at this school. We both agreed that you're making good progress in the classroom and how your teaching has inspired me to become a better human being.

19. THE CAR KEYS EXCUSE

I told Lassie to bury my Dad's car keys for a prank . . .

. . . Unfortunately Lassie misunderstood the prank and buried the car instead. She's an extremely obedient dog, pretty stupid, but obedient none the less.

20. THE FASHIONABLE EXCUSE

When I grow up I want to work in the fashion industry . . .

. . . Haven't you heard of being *fashionably late?* This is all good practise for my future career. I'll see you again at a fashionable time tomorrow.

21. THE NEW WORKOUT EXCUSE

I'm trying to get fit, so I tried a new workout . . .

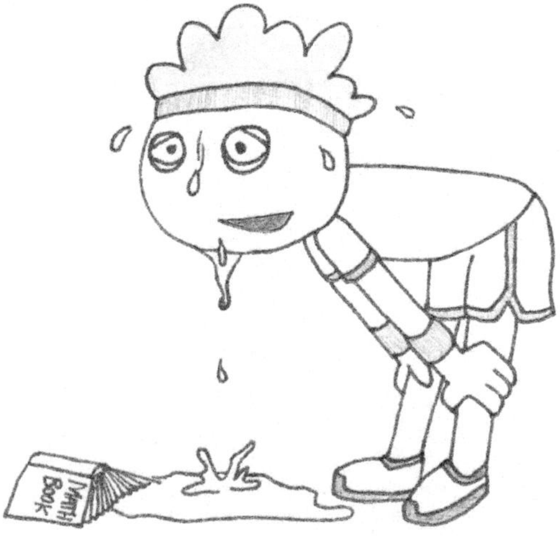
MATH BOOK

. . . I get dropped off 5 miles away from school with 5 minutes to go. I'm exhausted, I need to lie down.

22. THE TOAD KISSING EXCUSE

Sorry I'm late, but I had to give it a go . . .

. . . My dad read *The Princess & the Toad* to me last night so I spent all morning looking for my Prince. If you are wondering whether I found him, then the answer is no.

23. THE BREAKFEAST EXCUSE

My mum says that breakfast is the most important meal of the day . . .

. . . So I made sure I ate as much as I could this morning; I had a *breakFEAST*. It took me a while to roll all the way to school, which I personally think should not have been built on a hill.

24. THE WRONG SPECTACLES EXCUSE

My dad has terrible eyesight, and my eyesight is even worse . . .

. . . So this morning my dad accidentally took my glasses to work. Which meant that I had to walk to school wearing his glasses! Am I in the right class?

25. THE CAR SWAP EXCUSE

I decided to use my brother's car to get to school this morning . . .

. . . My little brother's car has 2 leg power, 4" plastic alloys and is extremely energy efficient.

26. THE LATE DAY EXCUSE

But don't you know? Did nobody tell you? . . .

National Late
for School Day

. . . It's *National Late for School Day!*

27. THE DANCING SHOES EXCUSE

I decided to wear my tap dancing shoes to walk to school today . . .

. . . I accidentally tap danced my way into an audition for the local production of *Hairspray the Musical* and have been given the lead role of Tracy Turnblad. By the way, rehearsals are 7am - 10am for the next 8 weeks.

28. THE HOME TUTOR EXCUSE

Did my parents forget to tell you, I'm being home-schooled . . .

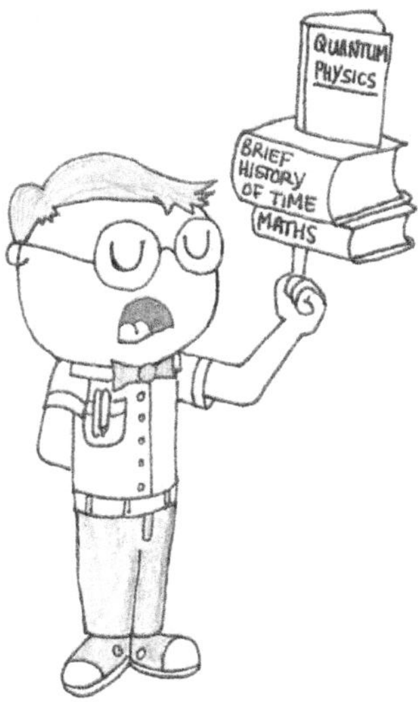
QUANTUM PHYSICS
BRIEF HISTORY OF TIME
MATHS

. . . From 6am to 9am my tutor, Professor Charles Einstein Shakespeare, teaches me advanced mathematics and quantum physics. What did I miss? The six times tables? I think I'll be fine then.

29. THE PRESENT EXCUSE

Sorry I am late, but there was a queue at the Flower Shop . . .

. . . I bought them to apologise for being late to class yesterday. I guess I'll have to buy an even bigger bunch of flowers tomorrow morning.

30. THE BUMP ON THE HEAD EXCUSE

I bumped my head when I woke up this morning . . .

. . . My mum told me that when I bump my head I should lie down for 5 minutes. Maybe I should stop sleeping in a bunk bed.

31. THE HELPING OTHERS EXCUSE

Well, this time I was late for purely unselfish reasons . . .

. . . I helped an old lady cross the road, I saved a cat from a tree and I deweeded the school garden. If there is anything else I can help you with let me know and I'll do it tomorrow morning.

32. THE HYPOCHONDRIAC EXCUSE

I'm feeling very well this morning . . .

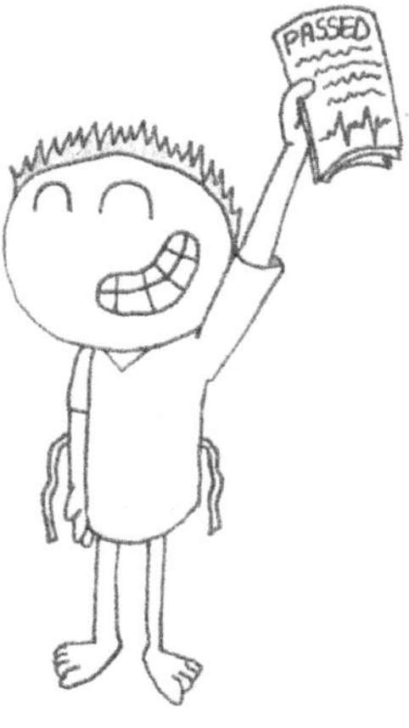
PASSED

. . . So well, in fact, that something *MUST* be wrong! Don't panic though. I did an extremely thorough 3 hour diagnostic test on myself this morning and, good news, I'm as healthy as a celery stick.

33. THE HOMEWORK EXCUSE

I was halfway to school when I realised I forgot my art homework . . .

. . . I spent all weekend working on it. I had to go back to get it. It's my design for a new school building made entirely of matchsticks and chewing gum.

34. THE DOG WALKING EXCUSE

I decided to take the dog for a morning stroll before school . . .

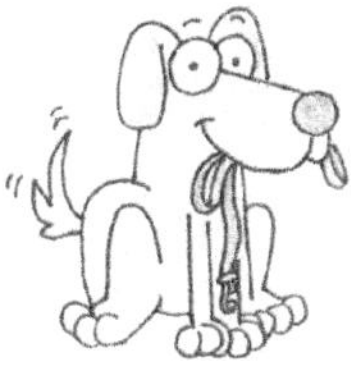

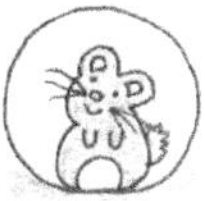

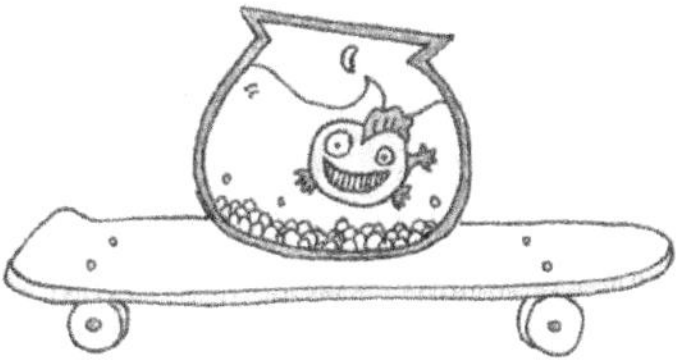

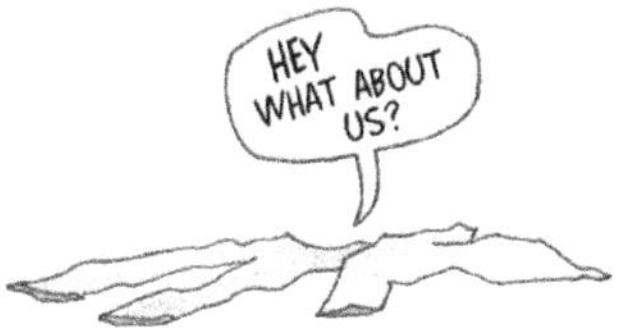
HEY WHAT ABOUT US?

. . . When I got back my hamster looked jealous, so I took him for a roll about. Then when I got back the goldfish looked jealous, so I took him for a walk on the skateboard. Then when I got back my pyjamas looked jealous, so I put them back on and had a quick snooze.

35. THE LOST EXCUSE

I took a different route to school this morning . . .

. . . I did get very very lost, but I did walk past a flower shop, a card shop and a big cuddly bear shop. These are for you.

36. THE SUBWAY EXCUSE

The subway made me late . . .

. . . By that I mean the subway train was late, not that I was stuck in a queue at Subway ordering a foot-long sub.

37. THE EARLY BIRD EXCUSE

Wait, before you tell me that I am late . . .

. . . I am actually really, really early for tomorrow. See, I brought my geography, history and maths books ready for tomorrow's lessons.

38. THE OPPOSITES ATTRACT EXCUSE

I am looking for a boyfriend who is intelligent, has wonderful hair, and is always on time . . .

. . . My mum told me that 'opposites attract'. So I've stopped doing my homework, combing my hair, and started to turn up late for everything. By the way I've got a Dentist Appointment at 2pm so I'll need to leave class at 2:30pm sharp.

39. THE BIRTHDAY EXCUSE

I know I'm late, but I had to celebrate. Today is his 1st birthday . . .

. . . Happy Birthday Angus! My pet hamster's birthday wish was to spend the day with me and I granted it.

40. THE DROP OFF EXCUSE

Sorry I'm late, I was dropping my parents off at work . . .

. . . The traffic was awful this morning on the 'work-run'. I'm thinking I should invest in better transportation. How about a catapult?

41. THE BROKEN WATCH EXCUSE

Have you seen the weather outside?

. . .

. . . It's cloudy. My brand new watch is solar-powered which unfortunately means it only works in sunlight. Could someone tell me the time please? How late am I?

42. THE FROG-I-CORN EXCUSE

I was searching for a Frog-i-corn . . .

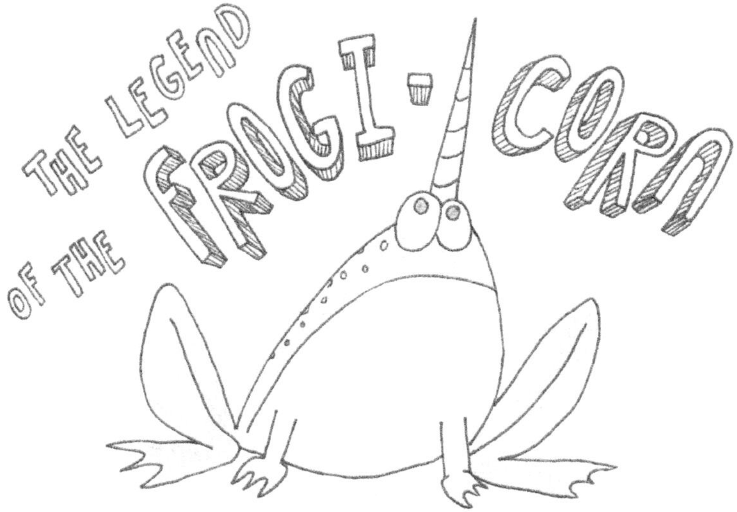
THE LEGEND OF THE
FROGI-CORN

. . . Have you heard *the legend of the Frog-i-corn?* They are half-frog, half-unicorn. They hide in children's bedrooms. They only eat lucky charms. And if you manage to catch a Frog-i-corn they'll grant you one wish.

43. THE NOT-SO-LATE EXCUSE

I don't mean to be rude, but . . .

. . . According to my watch it seems to me that everyone else was early this morning.

44. THE TIME EXCUSE

Look at all of you idiots, scurrying about like little ants . . .

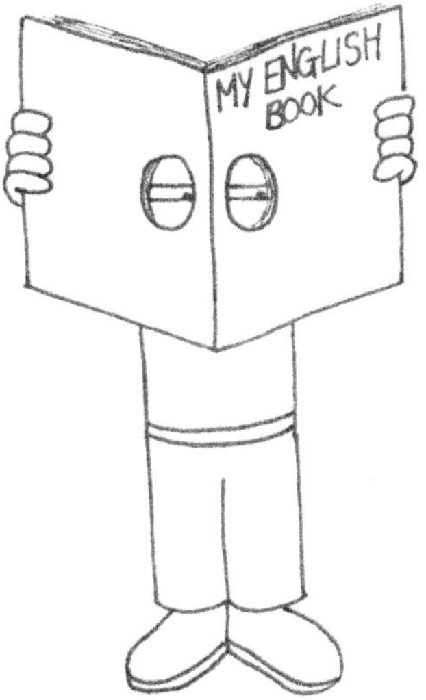
MY ENGLISH
BOOK

. . . Not me, I've seen the light. *Time is an illusion.* I have found the key to unlocking the handcuffs of the mind. Join me, and you too can be free from the sands of time.

45. THE SNAIL CROSSING EXCUSE

Have you heard of the latest eco-friendly scheme . . .

. . . The council have made this snail crossing on the cyclepath. I was waiting for 15 minutes for a family of snails this morning, but I'm glad the snails can cross the path without the fear of being squished.

46. THE LOST MY GLASSES EXCUSE

I couldn't find my glasses this morning . . .

. . . Which then meant I got on the wrong number bus, went to the wrong school and spent the morning learning how to make a pottery bowl.

47. THE LATE PASS EXCUSE

Late? I know I'm late, and here's your proof . . .

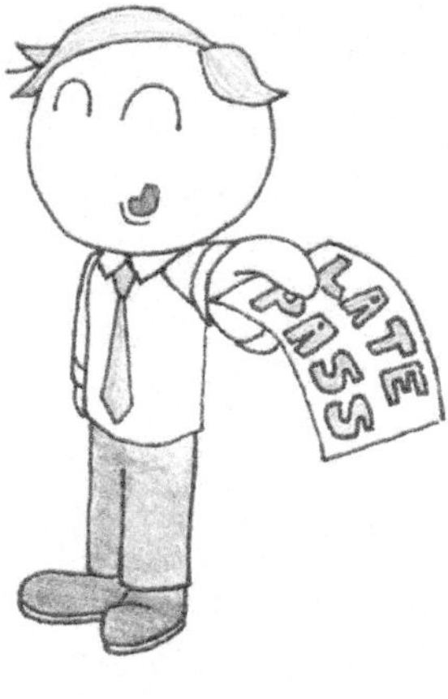
LATE
PASS

. . . It's my late pass. The Headteacher gave it to me. It's a new school scheme for forgetful pupils, like me

BONUS: TOOTHBRUSH ACCIDENT EXCUSE

I'm sorry for being late but I had to go to hospital . . .

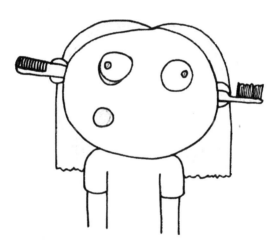

. . . After a sleepless night I kept missied my mouth when brushing my teeth this morning. The doctors said that they can't remove the toothbrush without causing permanent brain damage, but on the bright side my ears are minty-fresh and plaque-free.

48. THE GRIEVING EXCUSE

Sorry, I've had an emotional morning . . .

. . . I was at my friend's grandad's brother's granddaughter's neighbour's pet fish's funeral. Yes, it was very tragic.

49. THE RUN-OUT EXCUSE

I've officially run out of excuses . . .

. . . So therefore I, [insert your name here], apologise for my lateness and I promise to try my best to get to school earlier tomorrow.

Tips to help you get to school early:
1. Set your watch 10 minutes fast
2. Buy a jetpack
3. Brush your teeth in the shower
4. Invent a time machine
5. Get up earlier

BONUS: SAVING YOUR PET EXCUSE

I know I'm really late, but I had to save my pet goldfish . . .

. . . It may have looked like she was fine to the average pet owner, but I knew that Cassie the goldfish was either drowning or overdosing on water. I'll now have to go take her to the vet right away.

55

BONUS: TAKE OUT EXCUSE

I fancied an authentic Chinese takeaway . . .

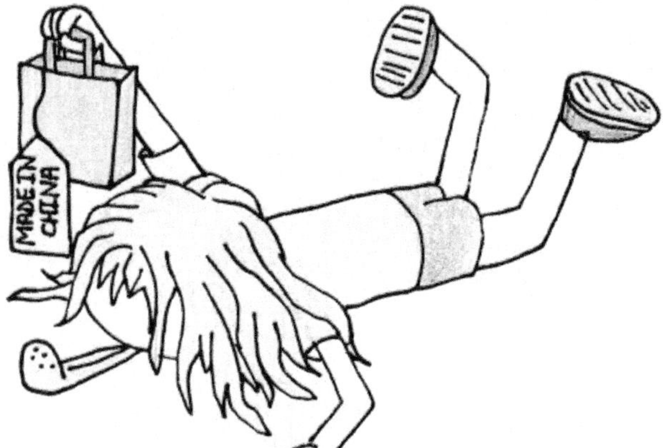
MADE IN
CHINA

. . . Do you know how far away China is? It was a 8,500 mile trip! So, what have I missed over the past two months?

BONUS: SICK BED EXCUSE

My bed told me that it was feeling very sick this morning . . .

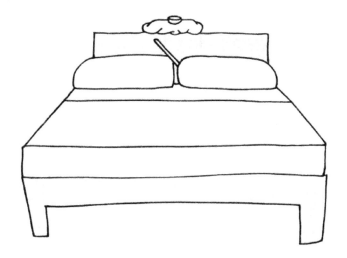

. . . So, I had to stay home and look after it.

BONUS: IMPORTANT SEMINAR EXCUSE

I know that I'm late, again . . .

REVOLUTIONARY TIME-KEEPING DEVICE

TIP SHEET (WHICH WILL TAKE 10 HOURS TO READ)

. . . but I want you to know it was because I was attending a seminar called 'How to Organise Your Time So That You Are Never Late Again'.

BONUS: BUTTERFLY EXCUSE

Erm, why am I late? . . .

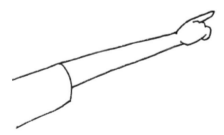

. . . Well, you know the butterfly flapping it's wings thing? That's why I'm late.

BONUS: LAZY SLOB EXCUSE

It may look like I don't care . . .

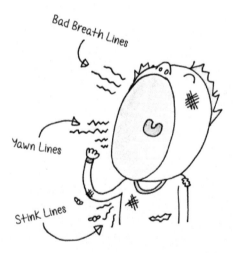

Bad Breath Lines

Yawn Lines

Stink Lines

. . . But I am trying extremely hard to be a living, breathing and smelly example to how your life could have turned out to be much, much worse.

BONUS: HARRY 'LATE FOR CLASS' POTTER EXCUSE

Ahhh drat! I was hoping that if I turned up late for class dressed as Harry Potter . . .

. . . you, my favourite teacher, would transfigure from a cat into Professor McGonagall and then threaten to turn me into pocket watch. I'll have to try it with all the other teachers as well, of course.

BONUS: TREE EXCUSE

Erm, why am I late? . . .

. . . Well, you know the tree falling in the woods thing? That's why I'm late.

BONUS: IMAGINARY FRIEND EXCUSE

It's not me who is late, it's my imaginary friend . . .

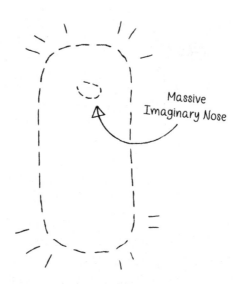

Massive Imaginary Nose

. . . It took her one hour and thirty minutes to powder her nose this morning. Don't worry, I'll have words with her.

BONUS: RAT TRAPS EXCUSE

I'm sorry for being late, but this one is a great excuse . . .

. . . An army of ants moved into my bedroom over the weekend. Pest Control have come and covered the whole house with rat traps so it took me a long time to navigate my way to the front door.

BONUS: EMAILS EXCUSE

I was late to school this morning for a very good reason . . .

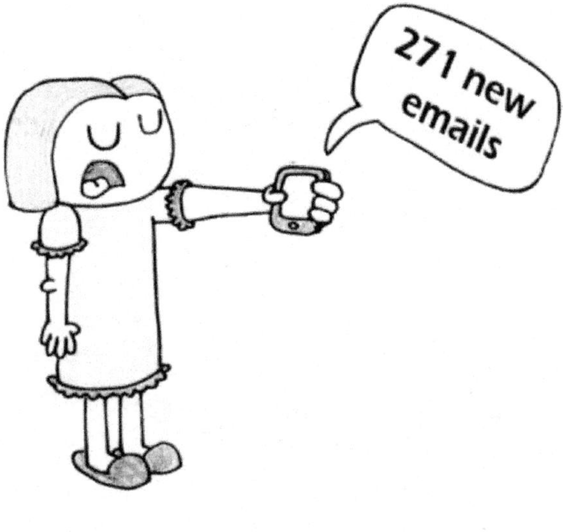
271 new emails

. . . As you can see I currently have 271 new emails. I started the morning with 2,389 emails. I really need to unsubscribe from some of the marketing email lists.

BONUS: POOL EXCUSE

Hang on . . .

. . . I thought you said we were meeting at the 'pool', instead of 'school'. Anyone got a change of clothes?

BONUS: EMPTY TANK EXCUSE

I was late because the car run out of fuel . . .

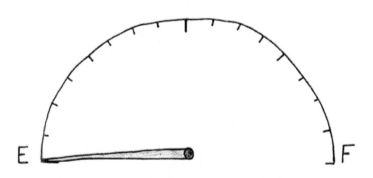

. . . Turns out the 'F' stands for 'Full' and not 'Fast-Mode' and the 'E' stands for 'Empty' and not 'Eco-Mode'.

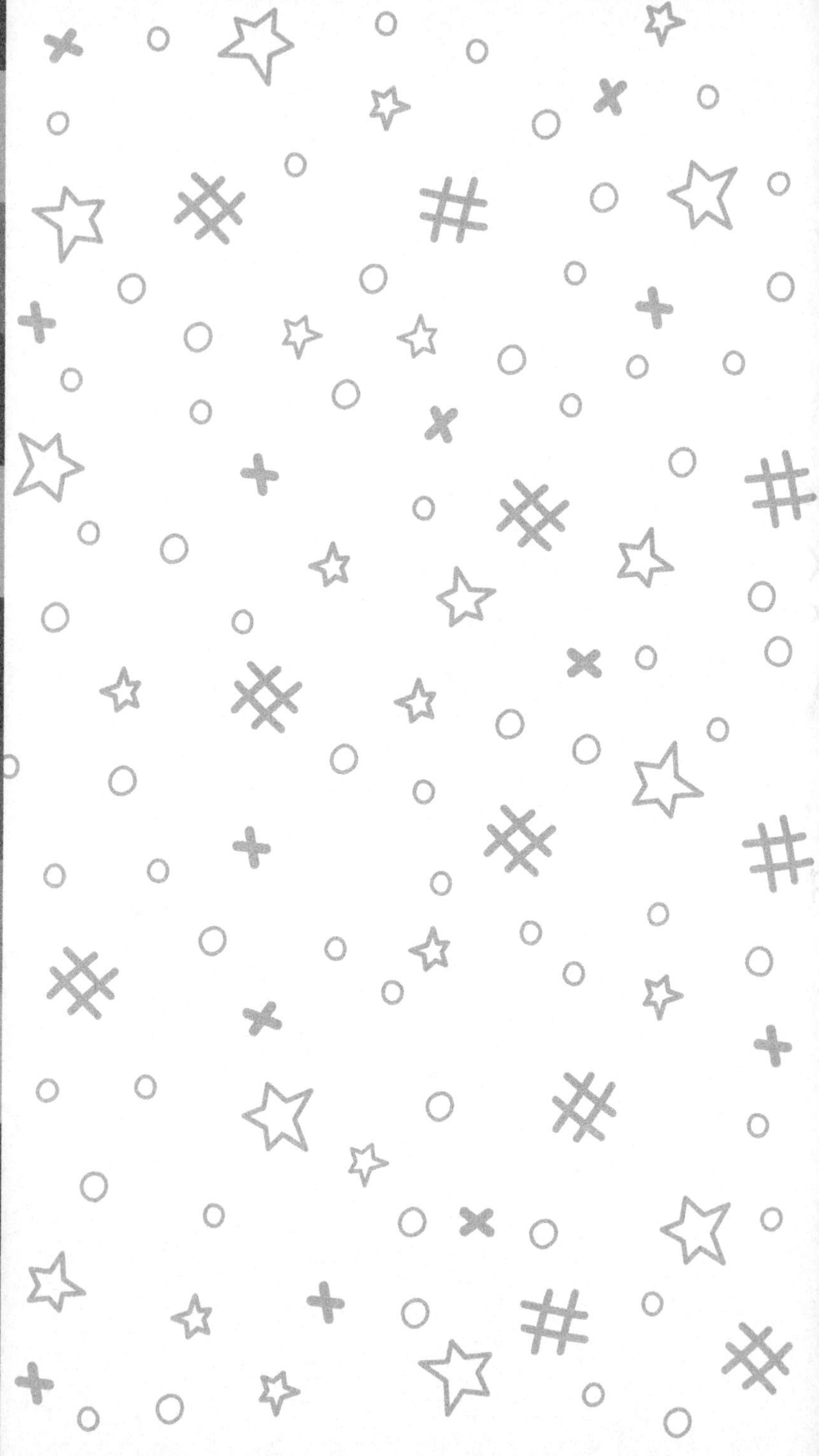

ABOUT THE AUTHOR

James Warwood is a writer and illustrator who lives on the borders of North Wales with his wife, two sons, and cactus (called Steve the Cactus).

He has a degree in Theology, which at the time seemed like a great idea, until he released he didn't want to become an RE Teacher. Instead, he writes laugh-out-loud middle grade fiction and non-fiction. He also fills them with his silly cartoons. He is the bestselling author of the EXCUSE ENCYCLOPEDIA and the TRUTH OR POOP SERIES.

James likes whiskey, squirrels, reading silly books, playing his bass guitar, and Greggs Sausage Rolls. He does not like losing at board games or having to writing about himself in the third person.

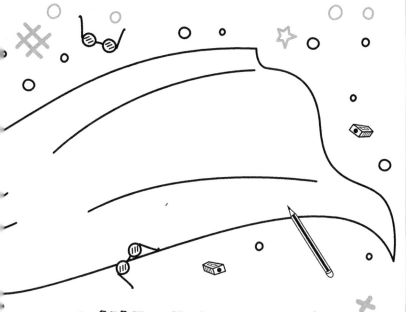

WHERE TO FIND JAMES ONLINE

Website: www.cjwarwood.com
Goodreads: James Warwood
Instagram: CJWarwood
Facebook: James Warwood

Want to join the
BOOKS & BISCUITS
CLUB?

Scan me to sign up
to the newsletter.

SO, WHAT'S NEXT?

CATASTROPHE
ONE MILLION SOCKS
VANQUISHED
DRAGON

MIDDLE-GRADE STAND-ALONE FICTION

The Chef Who Cooked Up a Catastrophe
The Boy Who Stole One Million Socks
The Girl Who Vanquished the Dragon

TRUTH or POOP?
TRUTH or POOP?
TRUTH or POOP?
TRUTH or POOP?
TRUTH or POOP?

TRUTH OR POOP SERIES

True or false quiz books.
Learn something new and laugh as you do it!

FORTY NINE EXCUSES FOR BAGGING MORE CANDY AT HALLOWEEN

THE EXCUSE ENCYCLOPEDIA

11 more books to read!

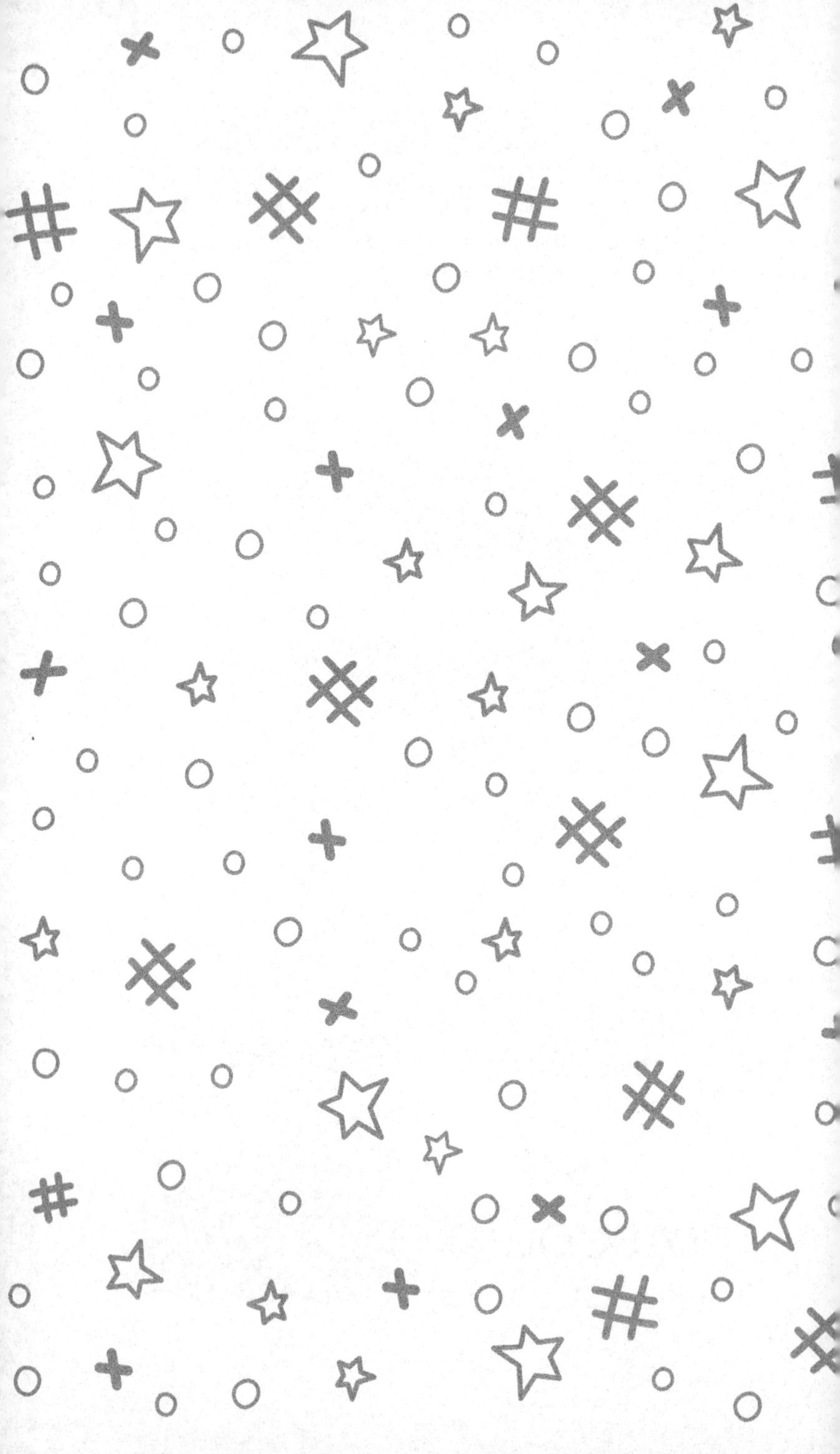

Printed in Great Britain
by Amazon

34083185R00046